AWARENESS EXERCISES FOR

FAMILY THERAPY

◆ MY FAMILY ◆ MY SELF ◆

Second Edition

AWARENESS EXERCISES FOR

FAMILY THERAPY

◆ MY FAMILY ◆ MY SELF ◆

Second Edition

IRENE GOLDENBERG
U.C.L.A. Neuropsychiatric Institute

HERBERT GOLDENBERG
California State University, Los Angeles

BROOKS/COLE PUBLISHING COMPANY
Monterey, California

Brooks/Cole Publishing Company
A Division of Wadsworth, Inc.

Printed in the United States of America

10 9 8 7 6 5 4 3 2 1

RC488.5.G64   1985   616.89'156   84-21387

ISBN 0-534-04687-8

Sponsoring Editor: Claire Verduin
Cover Design: Vernon Boes
Production: Barbara Kimmel

PREFACE

This journal is meant to accompany the second edition of <u>Family Therapy: An Overview</u> by Irene Goldenberg and Herbert Goldenberg (Brooks/Cole Publishing Company, Monterey, California, 1985). Our primary purpose is to enhance the learning process and make it more personal to you who are discovering how best to help troubled families. By relating the exercises found in each chapter to your own life, we hope to enliven and make more real and immediate what you learn in the textbook. The journal provides ample material for classroom discussion and, what is perhaps even more important, will lead you to look at yourself, your family, and the rules and dynamic interplay of family life in general. Ultimately, we will be delighted if the journal helps you to gain a family-systems perspective in your future professional work.

Each chapter of this personal journal contains suggested exercises tied to the material presented in the textbook's corresponding chapter. Our intention is to stimulate you to translate what you are reading into more personally meaningful terms. Here we ask you to look at yourself from a family systems perspective -- your family roles, the covert as well as the stated rules by which you were raised, your family of origin's power structure and ways of communicating, your family's ways of dealing with stress and crisis, the subsystems that exist or have existed in your family, and lots more. By doing so, we believe you will learn a great deal not only about yourself but also about family therapy at both a cognitive and an emotional level.

Beyond learning another set of theoretical concepts or therapeutic techniques from the text, we anticipate you will learn from this completed journal how your own family's dynamics and transactional patterns helped shape your individuality. Such self-knowledge should prove especially valuable when, as a family therapist, you become a participant in the family system of your client family, while being careful to avoid being drawn into entangling and thus compromising alliances and coalitions within that family.

Overall, we hope the text and journal will produce a synergistic effect, each enhancing the other, and that together they will facilitate the learning process for you.

Irene Goldenberg
Herbert Goldenberg

CONTENTS

CHAPTER 1

PATTERNS OF FAMILY INTERACTION

1.1. Dyads represent temporary or permanent liaisons between people. Within a family, numerous alliances of this kind occur, some lasting a brief period (e.g. during the temporary absence of a key member) and some more or less permanent. List the important dyads in your family. Pay particular attention to ones in which you have participated and to their significance in your adult life.

1.2. Were there any significant triadic or three person relationships when you were growing up? Following the format of Exercise #1, discuss their impact on your life.

1.3. How does making the paradigmatic shift from an individual to family perspective change the way you view relationships in your family of origin? Does the notion of circularity affect any long held linear ideas of who did what to whom?

1.4.   No families are problem-free; no individual grows up un-
        affected. In what ways would you consider yourself to
        have grown up in a "troubled" family? What were the negative
        consequences for you or each of your siblings? Were there
        any positive consequences for any family member? What
        were they? For whom?

1.5.   At different stages of a family's life cycle, different
        members may be labelled the "identified patient" or
        symptomatic person. Did this occur in your family? Who
        was so designated? Did you ever receive that designation?
        How did it affect your everyday behavior and your picture
        of yourself?

1.6. In what type of family did you grow up -- nuclear, blended, one led by a single parent? Did divorce play a role in your life? If so, what impact did remarriage, step-parents, step-siblings, separation from biological parent, etc. have on your upbringing and subsequent personality development?

1.7. What is your present family structure? Living at home? In a dorm? An apartment off campus? Cohabiting? Examine your own roles. In what ways are they similar to your parent's of the same sex? In what ways different? Did you tell yourself, growing up, that you would seek different patterns (e.g. male-female relationships) than you saw between your parents or between your grandparents? If so, how are they different? Any resemblances you hadn't anticipated?

1.8.   Describe the expectations you have about the family structure
        you will be part of in five years? Twenty years? Forty
        years? Include a discussion of your attitudes toward
        marriage, children, divorce, extended families.

1.9.   Chart your family's life cycle from a developmental point
        of view. Pay particular attention to any "stuck" places
        in the cycle where unexpected events (e.g. financial reverses,
        prolonged illness, an unexpected death) led to particular
        family problems. What were these problems? Did "symptoms"
        develop in any family member (e.g. depression, drinking,
        anxiety attacks)?

1.10. List in order of importance the roles tnat you currently
       play (e.g. son or daughter, friend, student, lover, neighbor,
       etc.).

       1._____   4._____

       2._____   5._____

       3._____   6._____

1.11. Which of these roles are integral to your sense of self
       (ones you believe you cannot do without)?

1.12. Of all the roles listed above, which _one_ would you insist
       on holding onto most strongly?

1.13. Of all the roles you have listed as currently playing, which would you find it most easy to give up?

1.14. Think of a current personal problem you have. What were the origins of that problem? What part, if any, did your family play in the development of the problem?

1.15.   What are the conditions that maintain that problem now?
        List:

1.16.   How do you see your current or future family of your
        own resembling or differing from your family of origin?

Same as Family of Origin   Different from Family of Origin

_____   _____

_____   _____

_____   _____

_____   _____

_____   _____

1.17.   What were the critical transition points for your family
        of origin (e.g. marriage, birth of first child, last
        child leaves home, etc.)? Was there one or more particular
        crisis points involving the resolution of any of these
        family tasks?

1.18.   How does your expected role (as a husband or wife or
        remaining unmarried) differ from your same sex parent?
        In what way were your social experiences growing up different
        or the same?

1.19. What "vertical stressors" or myths handed down from earlier generations, exist in your family? (For example, that childbirth is difficult, that men lose interest in their wives and look for other women during their 40's "mid-life crisis," that sex has to be tolerated but not enjoyed by a woman.) List some of your family's myths and discuss their impact on your development.

1.20. At what stage is your family in its life cycle? In what ways are the family's current problems typical and in what ways atypical?

1.21.   In many families, adolescents are the focus of much attention, as if they and not the family system are the center of family conflict. What was going on with your family members at the time of your adolescence that contributed to family harmony or disharmony.

1.22.   Choose a single parent you know. What are the major problems that person faces? What would be the major problem for you in that role?

1.23. How have economic factors affected your family?

1.24. Imagine your own death. What date do you estimate it
       will occur on? What will the funeral be like? How will
       other family members be affected?

1.25.   Draw a picture of your family. Be sure to include all
        members. After you have finished, note what you see
        about your view of relationships, alliances, coalitions,
        subsystems, etc., within the family.

1.26. How have racial or religious prejudices affected your life or the lives of your extended family? What would a counselor need to know about these issues if your family sought professional help?

1.27. Discuss with one or both of your parents the transition from one stage to another during their childhood and adolescence. Can they remember the problems they had? If applicable, how did your mother's life change when she lost one or both of her parents, or needed to care for elderly parents? What about your father's life under the same circumstances?

14

1.28. What kinds of relationships are maintained across generations in your family? Do grandparents maintain a special relationship in your family with their grandchildren? What is the significance of those relationships? Do they relate to separation issues?

1.29. Discuss the old joke that grandparents and grandchildren are friends because they have a common enemy in systems terms:

1.30. What was the impact of your family's socioeconomic and
       ethnic backgrounds on the development of your current
       attitudes regarding money, political affiliation, sense
       of acceptance in mainstream American society, etc.?

CHAPTER 2

FUNCTIONAL AND DYSFUNCTIONAL SYSTEMS

2.1. All families have family rules such as: no discussion
      about sex; deny mother's drinking; never raise your voice;
      if you can't say something nice about someone, don't say
      anything. What were some of the rules in your family
      of origin?:

2.2. What were some of the unspoken but agreed upon trade-offs between the adults in your family of origin? For example, that father will be logical and realistic if mother is feeling and sensitive.

2.3. How was money handled in your family of origin? Who decided what about it?

2.4. How will this way of dealing with money be different, or the same, in your own family? Why?

2.5. What homeostatic mechanisms do you recall operating in your family when you were a child? Do some still take place when you are together with your parents and siblings?

2.6. What homeostatic or corrective operations do you engage
      in now when dealing with a quarrel with a loved one?

2.7. How do you signal for attention with someone you care
      about? Verbally? Non-verbally? Is this tactic different
      or the same as you used as a child?

2.8. What kind of positive and negative feedback do you get
      from friends or current family members? Be specific.

2.9. Were you aware of subsystems that existed in your family
      when you were growing up? Describe them. Were they organized
      primarily by generation, gender, interest, or by a similar
      dimension?

2.10. How permeable was the parental boundary when you were growing up? What effect did the relative openness or closeness of your family system have on your development?

2.11. Consider fraternal twins born in 1970, one male, one female. Briefly distinguish the major differences in the socialization experiences they probably went through on the basis of gender differences.

2.12.   What are your reactions to a couple in a dual-career
        marriage? Could you see yourself in such an arrangement?
        Describe some advantages and disadvantages.

2.13.   According to Kantor and Lehr, families may be classified
        as open, closed or random. Which one did you personally
        experience as a child? Did you have a friend in a different
        type of family? How were his or her experiences different
        from yours?

2.14.   Where would your family of origin fit in Olson's circumplex
model? Select one of his 16 types of family systems
most like yours and explain your choice.

2.15.   Which of Reiss's family paradigms comes closest to the
pattern of your family of origin? Illustrate how they
dealt with a crisis, based on the type to wnich you have
assigned them.

2.16. How would you describe your family of origin on the following dimensions?

A. Expressiveness: Rate the degree to which this family system is characterized by open expression of feelings.

1	1.5	2	2.5	3	3.5	4	4.5	5

Open, direct
expression
of feelings

Direct
expression
of feelings
despite
some discomfort

Obvious
restriction
in the
expression
of some
feelings

Although
some feelings
are expressed,
there is
masking
of most
feelings

No expression
of feelings

B. Mood and Tone: Rate the feeling tone of this family's interaction.

1	1.5	2	2.5	3	3.5	4	4.5	5

Unusually
warm, affec-
tionate,
humorous
and optimistic

Polite,
without
impressive
or affection;
or frequently
hostile
with times
of pleasure

Overtly
hostile

Cynical,
hopeless
and pessimistic

25

2.17.   Discuss whether yours was a centripetal or a centrifugal
        family in their separation styles. Did each of your
        siblings use the same style in leaving the family?
        Explain.

2.18.   List those behaviors in your family which generally fall
        under these two headings:

Centripetal   Centrifugal

_____   _____

_____   _____

_____   _____

_____   _____

_____   _____

_____   _____

CHAPTER 3

EXPRESSIONS OF FAMILY DYSFUNCTION

3.1. Crises occur in all families. Some are resolved relatively
     quickly, others linger. Describe two such situations
     in your family -- one in which homeostatis was restored
     quickly, another in which resolution was more difficult.

3.2. In the more disruptive crisis mentioned above, what factors
     hampered resolution?

3.3. What experiences, if any, have you had with death in your
     family? Describe your reactions:

3.4. Referring to the above question, how did various members
     of your family adapt after one month? Three months?
     One year?

3.5. Has separation of one family member from the others in
     your family provoked a crisis? This can be due to illness,
     death, vacation, business, war, etc. What happened?
     How was homeostasis restored?

3.6. Discuss how two families of your acquaintance dealt with a death of a parent. Who was affected and how? How was the family restructured? How did the ages and stage of life of those involved affect the circumstances?

3.7. What do you see as the next developmental crisis for yourself (e.g. getting married, having a baby, divorce)? Discuss how your family structure will be affected?

3.8. Some crises are expected, others appear unplanned and
      unexpected. (For example, becoming a parent for the first
      time may set off a developmental crisis, while rape or
      sudden hospitalization may trigger a situational crisis,
      Can you compare your family's reactions to two such crises
      (one expected, one unexpected)?)

3.9. Healthy communication means that people can view the same
      event and understand it in the same way. Language and
      non-verbal communication may both be important aids in
      this process. Circle the dominant mode of communication
      in your family: Verbal--Non-Verbal. Who talks to whom?
      Is silence used as a form of communication? Illustrate.

3.10. "Disregard this notice" is a double-bind message. "Sex is dirty, save it for someone you love" is another. What double-bind messages have you been subject to?

3.11. Have you ever used mystification in communicating with your parents? What conflict were you trying to avoid by such a masking effort? How successful were you?

3.12. Have others tried to mystify you? Under what circumstances?
       How did it feel? What was the outcome?

3.13. Patterns of communication between people may be symmetrical
       or complementary (television situation comedies exaggerate
       these patterns). Describe a complementary pattern you
       have seen on a TV situation comedy. How are male and
       female roles defined? What conclusions about male-female
       relationships could you draw from this program?

3.14. Are you familiar with any film or TV series that shows a symmetrical relationship between a man and woman? Do they deal with the spiraling issue of symmetrical escalation? How? How are such conflicts typically resolved?

3.15. Would you define your parents as having primarily a symmetrical or complementary communication pattern? How did it enhance or constrict their relationship?

3.16.   What is your characteristic way of communicating with
        a member of the opposite sex? What role do you typically
        seek as most comfortable or familiar?

3.17.   Consider a family you have known that has a delinquent
        or psychosomatic child. How are the sub-systems organized
        within the family? How does the family deal with conflict?
        What homeostatic devices are activated when the child
        becomes ill or delinquent?

3.18. Do you know a family in which the parents, themselves immature, have reversed roles with one of their children, who has taken over the parenting role? Describe the relationships. Can you speculate on the future of the child who takes on parenting functions prematurely?

3.19. Scapegoats within a family go under many guises. Do you recognize any of these in your family?

idiot_____   mascot_____   wise guy_____

fool_____   clown_____   saint_____

malinger_____   black sheep_____   villain_____

imposter_____   sad sack_____   erratic genius___

Describe the behaviors of the persons labelled. What were the consequences later in life?

3.20.   Has physical violence ever erupted in your family? If
        so, what form did it take? How did the family members
        react? What mechanisms did the family call upon to stop
        the violent behavior?

3.21.   If violence has occurred, was drinking involved? What
        role has alcohol or other substances played in your family
        life?

3.22. Family myths help shape family interactions. What family myths helped shape your development?

3.23. Pseudomutual relationships are common in dysfunctional families. Think of a family in films or literature that uses pseudomutual behavior to maintain family homeostasis. What happens to the family members when they attempt to develop relationships outside the family?

CHAPTER 4

ORIGINS AND GROWTH OF FAMILY THERAPY

4.1. Safeguarding the personal privacy of the therapist-patient relationship has been a cornerstone of psycho-analytic treatment. Family therapy, on the other hand, is sometimes observed directly by others or videotaped for later viewing by trainees and supervisors or by professional groups. This brings up the issue of confidentiality. What are your feelings about participating with your family under the conditions of family therapy?

4.2. What are your feelings about sharing your "secrets" with your family members and a therapist? Any reservations? Any family taboo topics? How would you expect your parents to respond to these questions?

4.3. A 7-year-old child is doing poorly at school. How are each of the following systems affected?

Organ System (The Nervous System) _____

_____

Organismic System (The Individual) _____

_____

Group System (The Family) _____

_____

Organizational System (The School) _____

_____

Societal System (The Neighborhood) _____

_____

4.4 Referring to the previous question, offer your suggestions
     for positive intervention to change the situation.

4.5. Describe your own "world" in living systems terms. Be
      sure to comment on as many levels of subsystems in the
      hierarchy as you can in order to show relationships between
      levels (e.g. cell, organ, organismic, group, etc.).

4.6. Think of a problem in a family member, such as periodic despondency or bursts of aggressive behavior, and "explain" it at:
a. the individual level

b. the family level

c. societal level

4.7. Were any of the following patterns recognizable in your family of origin? Circle any that are applicable.

Marital skew   Marital schism   Emotional divorce

Discuss their consequences for all the members of your
family.

4.8. "Emotional divorce" was an adaptive technique that was
probably more common before actual divorce become easier.
What examples, if any, are you aware of in your family
history? Would that same adaptation occur today? If
not, why not?

4.9.   Although double bind messages occur in disturbed families,
        they also occur in normal ones. Can you give an example
        of a transaction from home, school or work where you were
        double bound? What did you do? What was the accompaning
        affect?

4.10.   Analyze some problematic behavior of yours (e.g. nail
        biting, smoking, over-eating, swearing) from an intra-
        psychic viewpoint and then a family therapy perspective.
        What has changed? Where is the locus of pathology?

4.11. Marital counseling was a precursor to family therapy.
      Did your family have or could they have profited from
      marital counseling? Which of the following personal
      problems might they have discussed?

           Spouse: marriage
           Child: relationship with child
           Other family relationship problems
           Job, school, or vocational problems
           Situational problems--death, illness, financial reverses

4.12. What are some of the problems and advantages you see
      associated with the multidisciplinary team approach to
      working with children?

4.13.   List the kinds of group therapy you have experienced
        yourself or known someone closely who has been involved

        Psychodrama_____

        Group therapy_____

        Human relations group--(T. Groups)_____

        Encounter groups_____

        Tavistock groups_____

        Others_____

        _____

4.14.   What positive and/or negative changes came from this
        experience?

4.15. What are your personal attitudes toward group or individual
therapy? Which would be better for you? Why?

4.16. Trace a conflict or problem you currently have back to
a grandparent.

4.17.   Trace a strength or skill you have in a similar way.

4.18.   Knowing yourself, if you were a therapist, which would
        you be: a conductor? or a reactor?   Why?

4.19. How effective would family therapy be with your family
of origin? Why?

CHAPTER 5

THEORETICAL PERSPECTIVES: PSYCHODYNAMIC AND RELATED MODELS

5.1.   Consider the classification system offered by the Group
        for the Advancement of Psychiatry, in which therapists
        are designated according to their theoretical orientation.
        In their scheme, Position A therapists work primarily
        with individuals (occasionally seeing a family) while
        Position Z therapists work exclusively with families.
        Many therapists take positions between these extremes.
        Where would you place yourself? Explain:

5.2.   The E-R-A Model differentiates family therapists according
        to their emphasis on Emotionality, Rationality or Activity.
        a. With which type would you and your family feel
           <u>most</u> comfortable?

        b. With which type would you and your family feel
           <u>least</u> comfortable?

        c. What would be <u>your</u> emphasis as a family therapist?

5.3.   Should family therapists emphasize the past or present,
        in your opinion? Explain:

5.4.   Classify yourself as a conductor or reactor type of person
        as described by Beels and Ferber. Discuss why you place
        yourself in that category. Think of someone you know
        who is the opposite of you. What are the advantages you
        see as a therapist for each position?

5.5.   Are you more influenced by emotionality, rationality or
        activity as described by L'Abate and Frey? How does your
        best friend or spouse operate? Is there a conflict?
        Discuss.

5.6. Consider the statement that an individual's capacity to successfully function as a spouse depends largely on that person's childhood relationships to his or her parents. Applied to yourself, what expectations might you have about your own marriage or other long-term relationships?

5.7. What "introjects" left over from early childhood relationships are you aware of in yourself today? What impact do such imprints have on:
a. current dealings with adults

b. current dealings with children

5.8. A woman resumes a career as her children enter high school. What potential failures in role complementarity may be expected? Discuss each member in a hypothetical family, emphasizing how each must modify existing roles.

5.9. Did any sudden role changes occur in any family member as you were growing up? What circumstances (e.g. death or disability of major wage-earner, widowed grandmother moves in) led to the change? Describe how the various members of your family were affected.

5.10. Choose a friend's family and describe any "interlocking pathology" between the parents that you have observed. How has your friend dealt with possible entanglements or side-taking? How successfully?

5.11. Try to imagine what it would be like to go to a therapist together with your parents or others in your family of origin.
a. What are your initial reactions?

b. What are your expectations of what would transpire?

c. Who would benefit most? Why?

5.12. If you presently are in a relationship that has developed
       problems, would it be better or worse if your spouse
       or significant other attended the session with you?
       Explain:

5.13. In your families ledger, what are some of the "unpaid
       debts" or restitutions that need to be made? If mother
       worked to put father through school, has she been repaid?
       Was there an imbalance in child-care responsibilities?
       Was that debt erased? If not, what are the residuals?

5.14. Family legacies dictate debts and entitlements. What legacies did you inherit? Were you expected to be an athlete, a musician, a scholar, a failure, beautiful, etc.

5.15. How have you carried those legacies or entitlements into your current relationships?

5.16.   How did those legacies conflict with those brought by
        your spouse or significant other to your relationship?

5.17.   Can you trace any of those legacies back to a grandparent.
        Discuss.

5.18. Robin Skynner calls unrealistic anticipations of others
       based on unfulfilled developmental needs (e.g. a lack
       of mothering) <u>projective systems</u>. People use spouses
       or children to recreate situations to satisfy these needs.
       Consider the mother who tries to make her child mother
       her -- or the husband who tries to get his wife to mother
       him. Are there situations like this that you can identify
       in your family? Describe:

5.19. Can you imagine what different experiences you would
       have if you and your family sought help from a) Ackerman
       or b) Bell? How would the sessions differ? With wnom
       would your family feel most comfortable at first? Later?
       Can you speculate on whose impact in producing change
       would be greater?

CHAPTER 6

THEORETICAL PERSPECTIVES: EXPERIENTIAL/HUMANISTIC MODELS

6.1. What does "psychotherapy as a growth experience" mean
     to you? Would that definition more likely invite your
     participation or make it less appealing?

6.2. How would your family react to a therapist's confrontational
      efforts to help them try to become more spontaneous and
      expressive of their feelings, both within the family and
      with outsiders?

6.3. Do you favor a therapeutic endeavor that attempts to uncover
      the past or one that addresses the immediate moment to
      moment encounter with an active and involved therapist?
      Explain.

6.4. What advantages and disadvantages do you see for yourself
      and your family in co-therapy?

6.5. Whitaker has been described in the text as iconoclastic
      -- and sometimes outrageous -- in dealing with families.
      He is unpredictable, and uses humor, his own fantasies
      and unconscious processes, even falling asleep, to contact
      and challenge his clients. How would you and your family
      respond to such an approach?

6.6. How would you feel about having your grandparents (separately or together) in a family therapy session with you and your parents? What special problems would arise? What problems would most likely be avoided? Who would be most helped?

6.7. Whitaker has a number of "rules" for "staying alive" as a human being and as a therapist, as described in the text. One is to "enjoy your mate more than your kids, and be childish with your mate." Was that true for your parents? Describe.

6.8. Following up on the previous question, briefly wnat were
      the consequences for the family members of your parents'
      interactions?

6.9. A Gestalt Therapist characteristically avoids taking a
      formal family history. What effect would that have on
      his or her understanding of your family? In your family's
      case, would it be better if certain historical material
      were known early on by the therapist, or not?

6.10.   Learning to communicate "I" messages is a basic exercise
        for Gestalt family therapy clients. For example, instead
        of an accusatory "You never pay attention to me!", an
        "I" message might be "I'm feeling ignored by you and
        it's upsetting me." Talk to a significant person in
        your life and be sure to make "I" statements. How does
        the transaction change?

6.11.   Which would be more comfortable for you and your family,
        a therapist who was self-revealing or one who was not?
        Why?

6.12. Virginia Satir classifies communication patterns in the following way:

Placater   Super-Reasonable   Congruent

Blamer   Irrelevant

Describe the members of your family of origin or your current family under each of these categories, paying particular attention to each person's characteristic way of interacting.

6.13. Single out a pair of individuals you know who are married. Observe which of Satir's patterns of communication seems to describe their way dealing with one another. Describe.

6.14.   Form a group of three persons in your classroom. Two
        strangers and yourself. Each person should choose a
        new first name. Then decide on a last name and assume
        a family role. Stay with your same sex role, but do
        not necessarily stay in your real life family (a son
        can be a father, etc.). Your communication snould be
        as follows:

        Pick a communication style and maintain it. If
        you are a blamer, begin each sentence with statements
        such as "You are never." "You are always."
        Find fault.

        If you are a placater, take the blame for everything
        that goes wrong. Make sure no one gets hurt.
        Never say what you want.

        The irrelevant one must not communicate in words
        properly. Be distracting.

        The super-reasonable one must be stiff and proper.
        Stick to the facts, ignore feelings or greet them
        with statistics.

Have a discussion for five minutes. Stop. Relax. Get
in touch with your body. What has happened in your new
family? How did it make you feel? Share your impressions
with one another and with the class.

6.15. Satir typically presents herself as a model of clear communication. She claims to tap the nourishing potential in each family through one or more of the following levels of access: physical, intellectual, emotional, interactional, contextual, nutritional, spiritual. To which would your family respond most positively? Which least? Explain.

CHAPTER 7

THEORETICAL PERSPECTIVES: THE BOWENIAN MODEL

7.1.   Where do you fit, in relationship to your family, on Bowen's theoretical Differentiation of Self scale? Remember that people at the low end are emotionally fused to the family and thus are dominated by the feelings of those around them. At the other extreme of the scale, the high end, people are able to separate feelings from thinking and thus retain autonomy under stress.

Place yourself on the scale below and explain your answer in the space provided.

| 1 | 25 | 50 | 75 | 100 |
| FUSION | | | | DIFFERENTIATION OF SELF |

7.2. What scores on Bowen's scale would you assign:
a. your mother?

b. your father?

c. your oldest sibling?

d. your youngest sibling?

7.3. Triangulation is often noted in the relationships between children. Can you remember a circumstance from your childhood when a third person was drawn into a relationship to decrease the intensity and stress between the dyad? What happened to the third person?

7.4. In your present family, does triangulation take place?
Who is the person most likely to be triangled in when
conflict arises between two other family members? Why?

7.5. Some of the ways Bowen suggests a family has of dealing
with tension are as follows: 1) increased emotional distance
between spouses; 2) physical or emotional dysfunction
in a spouse; 3) Overt, repeated but unresolved marital
conflict; and 4) Psychological impairment in a child.

Were any of these present in your family? Discuss.

7.6. Which of the children in your family, when you were growing
      up, was most fused to your parents? Can you speculate
      on why that particular child?

7.7. We all wish to differentiate appropriately from our families
      of origin, but sometimes we cut ourselves off emotionally
      or geographically from our families without resolving
      our emotional difficulties. Bowen calls this _emotional
      cut-off_. Has this occurred in your family? Describe.

7.8. Family therapists must differentiate from their own families
      of origin, according to Bowen, so that they do not, un-
      knowingly, become triangulated into the conflicts of some
      of the families with whom they work. With what kind of
      family would it be most difficult for you to work? Explain.

7.9. Following the premise in the previous question, with what
      kind of family could you most easily and objectively work?
      Why?

7.10.   Bowen's concept of the <u>multigenerational transmission</u>
        <u>process</u> includes the idea of the selection of a spouse
        with a similar differentiation level as one's own. Describe
        a family of origin and their offspring whom you know
        where you have been able to observe this process.

7.11.   What is your <u>sibling position</u> in your family of origin?
        How does it match the sibling position of the significant
        person in your life (spouse, roommate, lover, boyfriend
        or girlfriend)? For example, are you both oldest children
        who assume responsible leadership roles? Both youngest?
        One oldest, the other youngest? How do your corresponding
        sibling positions affect your relationship?

7.12.   Observe two pairs of friends with different sibling posi-
tions. How are their relationships influenced by growing
up in different birth orders in their families?

7.13.   Think about the birth order of your mother and father
in their respective families of origin. How influential
do you think this factor has been in determining the
nature of their relationship?

7.14.   There is a great deal of difference between a selfish
        person and a well-differentiated person. Think of two
        people who fall into these two categories. How are they
        different from one another? Elaborate.

7.15.   Observe an argument between two people you know. If
        you are drawn into the argument, attempt to remain in
        contact with both people, but remain emotionally
        disengaged. Observe how this changes the circumstances.
        Is it difficult to do? How do you feel about yourself?

7.16. Circle the term that best fits you when you try to
change a friend's behavior. Why?

      1. Coach   4. Counselor

      2. Therapist   5. Change Agent

      3. Family Counselor   6. Advisor

7.17. Framo brings family of origin members into his sessions
while Bowen is more prone to send clients home for frequent
visits, having coached them in their differentiation
efforts. Which would be best for your family? Why?

CHAPTER 8

THEORETICAL PERSPECTIVES: THE STRUCTURAL MODEL

8.1. Each family system is made up of a number of subsystems. List some of the subgroupings or coalitions in your family
a. by age:

b. by sex:

c. by outlook or common interest:

8.2. Which of the above bases for an alliance or coalition
      is most influential in determining how your family functions
      (i.e. carries out the day-by-day activities, communicates,
      negotiates differences, plans the future)?

8.3. List the subsystems in which you participate. How does
      your role differ in each?

8.4. Any conflict between subsystems in your family damaging or destructive to overall family functioning (e.g. older people dismiss what younger people have to say; females believe men are insensitive)?

8.5. Under stress, does your family become more enmeshed or more disengaged? Describe and explain the behavior consequences.

8.6.   Boundaries of a subsystem are the rules defining who
       participates and what roles each will play in the
       transactions necessary to carry out a particular family
       function. In a well functioning family, the parental
       subsystem is strong but flexible. How was the parental
       subsystem in your family?

8.7.   Power in a family is rarely absolute, but comes about
       through an alignment of forces. What person (or groups)
       had the most power in your family? Why?

8.8. Strong generational boundaries do not permit grandparents to take over parental functions. How did that operate in your family?

8.9. Discuss how you have "joined" or "accommodated" to a friend's or spouse's family that was different from your own?

8.10.   If you were to "restructure" the family system in which
        you grew up, what would be the most important change
        you would seek: change in rules, change in alignments,
        change in the distribution of power, etc?

8.11.   In growing up, most people think about wnat kind of parent
        they will be, and how they would do some things differently
        and some things the same as their parents. How would
        you be different from your same-sex parent (e.g. handling
        money, giving affection, imposing discipline)?

8.12. Following up on the previous question, how would you
       be the same as your same-sex parent?

8.13. Do your recognize any "dysfunctional sets" in your family
       of origin? How did these sets affect the family's response
       to a crisis or other stressful situations?

8.14. Reframing the meaning of certain behavior can provide
       a fresh perspective and make that behavior more
       understandable or acceptable. Reframe the following:
       a. Mother pokes into my private affairs too much.

       b. Father frightens the family when he drinks too
          much.

       c. Sister is selfish and only thinks of herself.

       d. Brother gets away with murder because he's the
          youngest child.

8.15. List some behaviors in a friend that are bothering you.
       Then try to reframe the meaning of the behavior so a
       new outlook results.

BEHAVIOR	REFRAMING
1) That girl is irritating me with her questions.	She would like to make contact with me.
2)	
3)	
4)	
5)	

8.16. How does the reframing in the previous question change
       your feelings about the bothersome behavior? Explain.

CHAPTER 9

THEORETICAL PERSPECTIVES: THE COMMUNICATION MODEL

9.1.   Communication takes place at both the verbal and non-verbal
       levels. Describe a recent incident in which you were
       involved where the message you received at one of these
       levels contradicted the message you were receiving,
       simultaneously, at the other level.

9.2.   List as many non-verbal expressions of interpersonal
       communication as you can (e.g. shrugging, finger
       pointing, grimacing).

9.3.   Every communication between people has a content/report
       and a relationship/command aspect. For example, Dad's
       comment, upon sitting down to dinner, that the salt is
       missing from the table, may also represent a command for
       Mom to go fetch it. Can you recall experiences between
       your parents where seemingly inocuous content messages
       also reflected commands?

9.4. Was the relationship between your parents primarily
symmetrical or complementary? Illustrate.

9.5. What sort of relationship definitions (symmetrical or
complementary) so you tend to get into with:
a. your male friends

b. your female friends

c. your parents

d. younger people

9.6. Haley believes that symptoms frequently are indirect strategies for controlling a relationship while at the same time denying one is voluntarily doing so (e.g. mother becomes ill when adolescent wants to leave for the evening). Any examples from your own experiences?

9.7. Observe a couple deciding an issue (e.g. division of chores, priorities for spending money) and describe what you learn about how each defines their relationship.

9.8.   Implicit in every relationship is a maneuver for power,
        according to Haley. How might you, as a family therapist,
        help a couple who is struggling with this issue?

9.9.   What unstated or covert rules existed in your family regarding
        taboo subjects (e.g. sex) or subjects everyone recognized
        but implicity agreed to avoid (e.g. a divorced aunt, a
        cousin in jail)?

9.10.   What would have occurred if anyone violated the rules
        described in your previous answer? Would an effort be
        made to silence or stifle the rule-breaker, change the
        subject rapidly, giggle, or what?

9.11.   Can you picture yourself, as a family therapist, "prescribing
        the symptom" for a family coming to you for help in order
        to change? How easy or difficult would it be? What
        special problems would arise for you?

9.12.   Paradoxical tasks are used by Haley and others when families
        are especially resistant to change. Can you imagine
        an area in your family's life where change might have
        been beneficial but was resisted by the family as a whole?
        How might paradoxical interventions by a therapist have
        helped?

9.13.   Suppose a friend of yours smoked too much, drank too
        much, or swore too much, and came to you for help in
        ridding himself of such excesses. Can you think of using
        a therapeutic double bind to aid in reducing or eliminating
        the symptom?

9.14.   What would your reaction be to a therapist wno used
        "prescribing" ("practice being depressed") or "restraining"
        ("go slow") as paradoxical techniques in working with
        you?

9.15.   Would "long brief therapy" as practiced by the Milan
        group be effective with your family of origin? What
        would be its advantages and disadvantages?

9.16. Any reaction to you and your family being observed behind a one-way mirror? How about the therapist leaving the room to consult with such observers periodically during the therapy session?

CHAPTER 10

THEORETICAL PERSPECTIVES: BEHAVIORAL MODELS

10.1. Select a family problem you have discussed earlier in
       this journal and restate the problem in behavioral terms.

10.2. Regarding the family problem you have now redefined in behavioral terms in the previous question:
a. Discuss its frequency and length?

b. What antecedent and consequent events are associated with the problematic behavior?

c. What environmental contingencies support and reinforce the behavior?

      d. Discuss the specific responses to the behavior by
        various family members.

10.3.   Think of someone with wnom you currently have a strained
      relationship. Speculate on the origins of the problem
      using behavioral concepts.

10.4. Following up on the previous question, what suggestions
       can you make for reshaping the interaction so that it
       becomes more positive and satisfying to both of you?

10.5. Try to shape someone's behavior by giving him or her
       positive reinforcements (a smile, a kiss, a gift,
       attention) whenever the desired behavior occurs, while
       ignoring undesired behavior. Continue to do this for
       seven days. Describe your results and draw conclusions.

10.6. Both Jackson and Stuart use the phrase "quid pro quo" (something for something) to describe how couples in a successful marriage work out a suitable arrangement for exchanging pleasures. Take a look at your parents (or an aunt and uncle) and try to describe the range and frequency of reciprocal positive reinforcements they exchange.

10.7. Would a contingency contract have been helpful in resolving any conflict you may have had with your parents when you were an early adolescent? Explain the problem and set up a contract.

10.8.   While the exchange of positive reinforcements between
        intimates sounds ideal, many people have trouble taking
        the "positive risk" of giving such a reinforcement before
        receiving one. What difficulties would exist for you
        in such a situation?

10.9.   Create a "caring day" list with a significant other in
        your life. Be specific in your requests and ask the
        other person to be the same in his or hers. Exchange
        the lists. After one week, note any changes in both
        of your degrees of commitment to the relationship.

10.10.   Were there any surprises in the list you received of
         "caring day" requests from your significant other?
         How did such surprises alter your perception of the
         relationship and/or change your behavior?

10.11.   What children's problematic behavior in your family
         (e.g. eating, sleeping or disciplining) might have been
         handled more successfully (or with less stress) if your
         parents had received behavioral parent training?

10.12. Did your parents use informal methods of reinforcing
        desired behavior (e.g. promising a bicycle if your grades
        improved significantly)? How well did such methods
        work? Any problems?

10.13. Establish a contract between yourself and a family member
        or friend. Begin by determining a common problem between
        the two of you, then negotiate a solution. Provide
        for reinforcers and negative consequences which are
        acceptable to both of you. Describe your problem,
        procedures, and results.

10.14. Set up a contract check list between:
a. a teacher and second grade pupil

b. a parent and teen-age son

10.15.   Would a couple you know who is contemplating seeking
         help for a sex problem feel more comfortable with a
         behavioral or systems approach? Explain.

10.16.   Discuss how you would feel in the role of behavior
         therapist as opposed to strategic therapist.

CHAPTER 11

THE PROCESS OF FAMILY THERAPY

11.1. List the major differences between individual and family therapy:

INDIVIDUAL THERAPY   FAMILY THERAPY

1) intrapsychic conflicts   interpersonal conflicts

2) _____

3) _____

4) _____

5) _____

6) _____

7) _____

11.2.   Describe two people you know who need help. Would you
        recommend them for family or individual treatment? Explain
        why.

11.3.   Under what conditions would you treat a marital or sexual
        problem with only one member of the family?

11.4.   Describe a family situation you have observed where family
        therapy is not indicated.

11.5.   Do you have a friend who is undergoing an "inter-
        generational conflict" with his or her parents? How
        would family therapy help?

11.6.   What topics (extramarital sex, incest, etc.) do you think
        cannot be discussed in a family setting? Why?

11.7.   If your family were to come for family therapy, would
        you want the therapist to take a history? Why or why
        not?

11.8.   If your family were to come for family therapy, would
         you want the therapist to diagnose them? If yes, should
         he or she share that diagnosis with the family? If no,
         why?

11.9.   Observe a family planning something they can do together
         as a group (go to a movie, vacation, etc.). How much
         information can you gather about the power structure,
         communication patterns, and degree of family functioning?
         Discuss.

11.10.   Look at the structure of the place where you work or
          go to school. Would you characterize the climate as
          rigid or flexible, autocratic or democratic, competitive
          or cooperative? How does this affect your functioning?

11.11.   What values do you hold that might affect your functioning
          as a family therapist?

11.12. Make a genogram of your family, covering at least three
        generations.

11.13. What have you learned about relationships within your family from the genogram? Does seeing it on paper help clarify any family issues?

11.14. A major ethical concern in family therapy is whose interest the therapist should serve. The identified patient? The family? Only the members attending the sessions? Discuss your viewpoint.

11.15.   In your opinion, how old does a child have to be to
         be involved in a family session? Why?

11.16.   Termination of a personal relationship or a therapeutic
         one is often difficult. What are the problems you might
         expect and are there any special difficulties you might
         have terminating family therapy?

CHAPTER 12

INNOVATIVE TECHNIQUES IN FAMILY THERAPY

12.1.   In your class, pick a group of people to represent your
        family. Place them physically to show their relationship
        to one another. Discuss that with the class. Change
        their positions to show how you would like them to be.
        What did you learn?

12.2.   Observe two people in a conversation about a neutral
        subject on videotape. Watch for communication through
        body language. Match it to the spoken communication.
        What can you say about the communication? (Use T.V. if
        videotape not available.)

12.3.   Observe the same two people discussing an emotionally
        charged subject. Discuss the communication pattern.
        Is there a change verbally or non-verbally?

12.4.   Turn the sound off on a television dramtic program or
        daytime soap opera. Can you identify any family choreo-
        graphy patterns that tell you something about the character's
        current interactions? Describe.

12.5.   If you have access to your family's home movies, observe
        them at different stages of the family life cycle and
        comment on any changes you may observe in the trans-
        action patterns.

12.6. Draw a floor plan of the home where you spent the longest time as a child. What memories are brought back about significant friends and relatives? Note your feelings as you carry out this exercise.

12.7.   Look at a family photo album and describe the development
        of gender identification in yourself or another family
        member over as many years as photos are available .

12.8.   You enter a clinic with a problem person in your family.
        Your family is in great distress. You are told you will
        have to commit yourself for 2 to 2 1/2 full days to solve
        the problem. Your whole family will have to do the same.
        What are some of the negative aspects of this for you?

12.9.   Regarding the simulated Multiple Impact Therapy experience
        in the previous question, what are the positive aspects
        you envision?

12.10. At what point in your life could you and your family
        have used brief (6 session) crisis intervention? For
        example, you might consider divorce, death, delinquency,
        drugs, alcohol, school separation, or an accident as
        possible crisis times. Describe the time and why you
        believe intervention might have been helpful.

12.11. How has divorce affected your family? At wnat point
        might intervention have helped? Why?

12.12. Can you think of problems your family attempted to resolve
        through first-order changes (within the existing system)
        when second-order changes (restructuring the system)
        were called for? Elaborate.

12.13. Brief family therapy, as practiced by the Palo Alto
        group, relies heavily on paradoxical strategies to
        help a family revise self-defeating solutions to a
        problem. Think of two such situations in your family:
        one where the time-limited approach utilizing the therapeutic
        paradox might have helped, the other where long-term
        efforts at improving the family's problem-solving skills
        would have been more effective.

12.14. Multiple marital couples therapy, like all forms of
        therapy, needs skilled facilitators. What do you see
        as the problems inherent in three couples getting together
        to talk aabout their problems without a leader? Would
        there be any advantages?

12.15.   Learning new patterns for resolving one's own personal
         conflict may come from observing another family or family
         member deal with an analogous conflict. Some non-therapy
         groups that make use of this principle are Al-Anon,
         a family support group for a member who is an alcoholic,
         or nursery school observation classes where mothers
         observe and then discuss their children's behavior.
         Another recent innovation, Marriaage Encounter, offers
         marital couples a chance to observe other married people
         solve their problems. Visit one of these programs and
         identify the potentials for change.

12.16.   A therapist has been seeing you and your family in her
         office. She suggests that she and her co-therapist
         visit you at home next session after dinner. What is
         your reaction? How will your family react?

12.17.   Your grandfather becomes seriously depressed. He lives
         with you and the whole family is upset. The therapist,
         who sees him, says he will not hospitalize him, but
         insists on working with the entire family. What are
         some of the pros and cons to this approach from your
         point of view? How would the members of your family
         feel?

12.18.   If you have participated in a social network group such
         as a dorm, religious group, sorority, boy or girl scout
         group, fraternal organization, cousins club, etc., describe
         what happens when the group turns its attention to the
         problems of one member.

CHAPTER 13

LEARNING, PRACTICING AND EVALUATING FAMILY THERAPY

13.1.   How have your personal experiences, family history, and
        schooling influenced whether you have an individually-
        focused or family-oriented view of the causes and treatment
        of maladaptive, problematic or dysfunctional behavior
        in an individual?

13.2. Try to determine what your personal objectives are as a family therapist. List them in descending order of importance.

1. _____

2. _____

3. _____

4. _____

5. _____

13.3. Compare your training in developing family therapy skills with others (members of the established mental health professions or graduates of programs designed to provide specific training in marital/family therapy). What do you see as the special benefits and shortcomings of each?

13.4.   A course on working with your own family is included
        in many training programs. Compare it to a therapist's
        personal psychoanalysis as an adjunct to becoming an
        effective family therapist. What are the advantages
        and disadvantages?

13.5.   Should a family therapist be required to have personal
        family therapy experience? Why or why not?

13.6. For you, which would be a better learning experience,
a single integrated approach to family therapy or sampling
a variety of family therapy techniques and theories?
Why?

13.7. Rate yourself on the following three skill dimensions
as discussed in the textbook:

Perceptual Skills

1	2	3	4	5	6	7

Do not do well.   Acceptable behavior   Very good.
One of my weak   in this area.   One of my
behaviors.   strong points.

Conceptual Skills

1	2	3	4	5	6	7

Do not do well.   Acceptable behavior   Very good.
One of my weak   in this area.   One of my
behaviors.   strong points.

Executive Skills

1	2	3	4	5	6	7

Do not do well.   Acceptable behavior   Very good.
One of my weak   in this area.   One of my
behaviors.   strong points.

13.8.   What are some of the advantages and disadvantages of
        going over a videotape of you with a family in supervision?

13.9.   Marathon experiences are available in our society in
        a number of forms: running marathons, encounter groups,
        est, religious retreats. What have you observed about
        yourself or others when they leave these groups? What
        happens 3 to 6 months afterward? What conclusions can
        you draw?

13.10. What would be your hesitations about having live
        supervision?

13.11. If you had live supervision, which would be most
        comfortable for you? Least comfortable? Why?

        1. Telephone call from supervisor who offers suggestions

        2. Bug-in-ear as you conduct session

        3. Supervisor enters therapy room

        4. Calling you out of room during a session for consultation
           with a team that has been observing you with your
           client family

13.12. Would you prefer to work in family therapy alone or
        as a co-therapist? Explain. If you had a co-therapist,
        what qualities would be important? Would the sex of
        your co-therapist matter? Why?

13.13. Would you refer your own family to a family therapist?
        Why or why not?

13.14.   Some families are more anxiety-provoking for some therapists than others. What kinds of families would be the most difficult for you?

13.15.   What kinds of families would you feel most comfortable with? Consider social class, family style, religion, and other factors.

13.16.   What aspect of family therapy would you like to continue
         to explore? Clinical methods? Theory? Or research
         on efficacy? Why?